Social Intelligence Skills for Law Enforcement Supervisors/Managers

Stephen J. Sampson, Ph.D.

HRD Press, Inc. • Amherst • Massachusetts

Published by: HRD Press, Inc.
22 Amherst Road
Amherst, MA 01002
800-822-2801 (U.S. and Canada)
413-253-3488
413-253-3490 (fax)
www.hrdpress.com

ISBN 0-87425-857-X

Production services by Jean Miller
Cover design by Eileen Klockars
Editorial work by Sally M. Farnham

Table of Contents

- Most people Today quit The
job b/c of The boss, not The
agency.

Acknowledgment

This Intervention Skills Model has been adapted from the Human Resource Development (HRD) model developed by Dr. Robert R. Carkhuff, Chairman of the Board of Directors, Carkhuff Institute of Human Technology.

This HRD model is copyrighted and any use of this material without the written permission of the copyright owner would be a violation.

We gratefully acknowledge the generosity of Dr. Carkhuff for his permission to adapt this material. Two resources provided the major framework for this manual:

- Blakeman, J. D., Pierce, R. M., Keeling, T., and Carkhuff, R. R. *IPC: Interpersonal Communications Skills for Correctional Management.* Amherst, MA: HRD Press, Inc., 1977.

- Blakeman, J. D., Pierce, R. M., Keeling, T., and Carkhuff, R. R. *IPC: Interpersonal Communication Skills for Corrections—A Training Guide.* Amherst, MA: HRD Press, Inc., 1977.

Preface to the Trainee

This is a skills-oriented course: no "shoulds" or "oughts," but practical, applicable skills that are immediately useful. The program is realistic. It is not designed to take issue with the fundamental law enforcement skills you have or will learn in your formalized training or that you receive from the tutoring of more experienced supervisors. It is designed to complement both of those: to **add** to your skills base so that when you **choose** to use it, it will be there.

Overview of the Learning Plan

The learning plan is both simple and systematic. First, the trainer will **Tell** you what the learning module is all about. Second, he or she will **Show** you the skill that will be learned in the module by demonstrating its use through the instructor demonstration and video simulation. Third, he or she will then have you learn the skill by **Practicing** it in a role-play activity. Fourth, and last, you will have **Input** into the learning both by evaluating the role player and then having an opportunity to discuss the activity thoroughly and give your thoughts and ideas based on your observations of the role play.

Like any training, failure can be programmed as well as success. The key to success is your willingness to participate fully in the written exercises, role plays, discussions, and sufficient practice. Good luck!

Introduction to the Intervention Skills Model

During this training segment, your trainer will preview the intervention skills model. He or she will explain that the skills to be taught come from the experiences of law enforcement officers just like yourself. He or she will then outline the model:

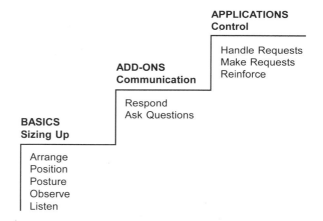

INTERVENTION
MODEL

APPLICATIONS
Control

Handle Requests
Make Requests
Reinforce

ADD-ONS
Communication

Respond
Ask Questions

BASICS
Sizing Up

Arrange
Position
Posture
Observe
Listen

EXPLANATION Traditionally, the training given to law enforcement supervisors has been aimed at their heads—it was filled with theories and ideas. Sure, there was some skills training, but that was usually in firearms or self-defense. Another thing about the training was that it was almost exclusively concerned with the technical aspects of enforcement. While these are obviously legitimate concerns, this orientation doesn't take into account the fact that law enforcement officers spend much (if not most) of their time interacting with people—and with each other.

Officers traditionally have been trained to keep the peace, but not necessarily to get along with people effectively. More important, they haven't been trained to get supervisees to do what the supervisor wants them to do without a hassle, which is what the job is really all about.

This training program is an effort to change that orientation. It's based on work done by trainers and researchers in the field of criminal justice over the past fifteen years. It's known as Human Resource Development. It's based on a careful study of the skills that truly effective officers demonstrate. Techniques for identifying those skills have been developed and now there are techniques for teaching others, like you, how to acquire and use those skills.

This training program is designed around the intervention skills model. A model is like a road map: It shows you where you're going. As you can see from the diagram on the previous page, the model has three major sections: the Basics, the Add-Ons, and the Applications.

The Basics
The **basics** are pre-management skills that give you information that helps you decide what action to take in any given situation. Another name for the basics is **sizing-up skills.**

The Add-Ons
The **add-ons** are communicating skills that will help you get a supervisee to explore and share information with you. These skills are the key to finding out what's really going on in a situation.

The Applications	The **applications** are skills that help you control behavior in a respectful way so that you get what you want done with minimal hassles.
	During this training program, you'll get a chance to learn about and practice all of these skills.
NOTE	Throughout this book, you will see blocks indicating "VIDEO." A DVD was developed as an additional training tool to accompany this book; it is available for purchase by going to our Web site:

www.hrdpress.com or
www.sotelligence.com

PRACTICE	Think back on your own experience of being managed. You've probably had supervisors or managers who you thought did a good job in managing you and others who you felt did a poor job. Think about the good supervisors or managers. What qualities or skills did they demonstrate that made them effective in managing you—that made them successful in motivating you to do a good job? List those qualities and skills below.

_____

_____

_____

_____

_____

_____

_____

Section I

The Basics:
Sizing Up the Situation

The basics are sizing-up skills that help you know what's happening in any situation. Sizing up helps you avoid costly mistakes and maximizes the chances that your decisions and actions will be effective and accurate. Sizing up works because it gets you ready to use information to manage and often prevent problems. Using the basics is always appropriate because every situation must be sized up.

INTERVENTION
MODEL

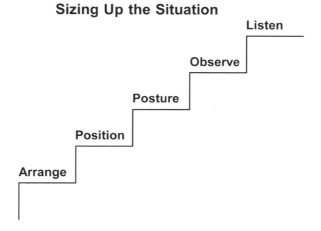

THE BASICS

Sizing Up the Situation

Listen

Observe

Posture

Position

Arrange

1

FIVE BASIC SKILLS Sizing up any situation involves five very basic skills:

1. Arranging
2. Positioning
3. Posturing
4. Observing
5. Listening

Why basic? The word *basic* is important here. The five skill areas are basic and fundamental to everything you will learn in Sections II and III of this manual—and to everything you actually do on the job. You cannot hope to communicate safely and effectively with a person or persons until you have used these skills to size up the situation. By learning to make continual use of these five basic skills, you can maximize your chances of making the right response in situations where a wrong response could be very costly indeed.

The five basic skills are cumulative in that each new skill builds on each previous one. For example, positioning effectively means that you should already have arranged your environment; posturing yourself effectively means that you should already have arranged your environment and be in an effective position; observing accurately means that you should already have arranged your environment and gotten into an effective position and posture; and so on. In other words, you don't simply use one skill at a time. Instead, you size up a situation by making maximum possible use of all five basic skills.

Getting ready In general, of course, the skilled supervisor always systematically sizes things up on his or her shift, whether responsible for traffic,

2

walking a beat, or being on patrol. Here are some ways a supervisor sizes things up before actually going on duty:

- Checks with the previous shift supervisor and reviews the prior shift activities to see what has happened during the last shift.

- Reads the log book of the supervisor he or she is replacing and asks for a briefing about the conditions of the area of responsibility.

- Determines if there are items that need priority attention.

It is in this final phase of pre-duty activity—and in the actual duty that follows—that the supervisor puts the five basic skills to maximum use.

PRACTICE   Why do you think that sizing up the situation is important?

_____

_____

_____

If you were to think about your responsibility prior to going on duty, what would you be thinking about?

_____

_____

_____

Which of the basic skills do you think would be most helpful for you to get that information?

_____

_____

_____

Arranging

How you arrange, or order, the environment in which you manage or supervise contributes to your goal achievement. If you are highly skilled regarding your interpersonal management skills, the arrangement of the environment will be somewhat overshadowed in importance by your skill level. However, if you regard your people management skills as only moderately effective, as is the case with most managers, then this is an area in which you should expend real effort.

When we examine the behaviors of highly functional professionals, one dominant trait they display is that they place a lot of significance and importance on details. Arranging sub-skills focus on the details of the environment.

INTERVENTION
MODEL

THE BASICS

Sizing Up the Situation

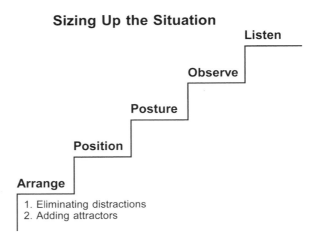

Listen

Observe

Posture

Position

Arrange

1. Eliminating distractions
2. Adding attractors

4

Arranging means eliminating from the environment anything that might distract you **or** the person who you are supervising or with whom you are interacting. A second goal of arranging is to make the environment pleasant, not stressful, by adding attractors.

Eliminating distractions. The first principle of arranging is eliminating distractions. Most people have worked in an environment where there were many distractions. Remember what it was like to try to perform your job effectively when you worked in a distracting environment? For both you and your supervisee, outside noises, uncomfortable chairs, and an uncomfortable room temperature can divert your attention and deplete your energy so that more time is required for each task and errors occur more frequently.

Imagine the work environment where you manage others. Are there noises that can be eliminated? Can phone calls be intercepted? Is furniture reasonably comfortable? Does the placement of furniture create a barrier? Or is it best to simply remove yourself and the person with whom you are talking from the distracting work environment, and talk with them in a quiet conference room? Eliminating those distractions is important to successful communications and interactions.

ARRANGING means eliminating from the environment anything that might distract you **or** the person you are supervising or with whom you are interacting.

VIDEO   **"Eliminating Distractions: The Wrong Way and the Right Way"**

5

PRACTICE List some distractions you experienced when you were in the presence of your supervisor or manager and communication was important.

_____

_____

_____

_____

_____

PART 2 OF ARRANGING **Adding attractors.** The second sub-skill of arranging is adding attractors. Following the elimination of distractions, you might consider actually adding *attractors* to the environment. You can enhance your work environment in order to manage and communicate more effectively. Providing privacy and comfortable furniture, and having refreshments may all facilitate your efforts. Your best standard is probably the one you would establish for yourself.

ARRANGING means adding
enhancements to the environment
that may lead to reduced stress and
more effective communication.

PRACTICE List the characteristics of a present or past environment that either contributed to reducing your stress or facilitated your ability to communicate with others.

_____

_____

_____

_____

_____

Positioning

Positioning means putting yourself in the best possible place to see and hear individuals or groups. This helps you see and hear what you need to in order to carry out your duties to protect yourself and to keep minor incidents from becoming major ones.

The three parts of Positioning are:

INTERVENTION
MODEL

THE BASICS

Sizing Up the Situation

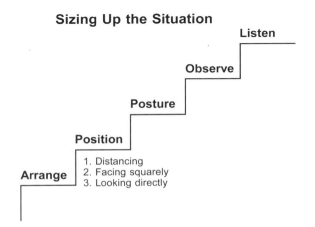

Listen

Observe

Posture

Position

1. Distancing
2. Facing squarely
3. Looking directly

Arrange

Physically positioning yourself in relation to an individual or a group is very important in managing people.

There are several different principles or activities that you may feel are important to effective positioning. The three basic parts of positioning that we will focus on in this section are establishing an appropriate distance, facing squarely, and looking directly.

As an effective supervisor, you need to position yourself where you can see and hear problems. Being in a good position helps you to observe what is transpiring and, therefore,

7

to resolve situations before they escalate into major problems. In addition, people who think they are not being observed are typically a problem because they tend to live by the rule, "We'll get away with as much as we can—or as much as you let us." Obviously, it's impossible for you to be everywhere at once. Yet the more you use positioning skills to see and hear, the less likely it is that the supervisees will become involved in things that are against the rules.

Positioning also communicates interest to supervisees that gives them a feeling that you care about their well-being.

Now, let's take a look at the three specific skills, or procedures, involved in Positioning: distancing, facing squarely, and looking directly.

PART 1 OF POSITIONING **Distancing.** The first principle of distancing is to be able to observe and listen to what you are managing. Of course, there will be many situations where you can't observe the supervisee (e.g., talking to the supervisee on the phone) or listen to the supervisee (e.g., you can see their actions but can't hear what's being said).

On the other hand, if a supervisee is in your office or talking with you in the hallway, choose a distance that enables you to observe and listen to him or her more effectively.

POSITIONING means distancing yourself close enough to see and hear the persons you manage if the situation allows for it and "safety" is not a concern.

PART 2 OF
POSITIONING

Facing squarely. Facing squarely, or fully, ensures that your position gives you the most effective line of vision. Your left shoulder should be lined up with the left boundary line of the area you are watching, and your right shoulder should be lined up with the right boundary line of the area you are watching. When you move your head to either side so that your chin is right above either shoulder, you should be able to see the entire field for which you are responsible.

POSITIONING means facing
a person, persons, or area
squarely if safety is not an issue.

See everything

Sometimes the size of the area for which you are responsible (e.g., a section of a community) makes it impossible to remain in one position. In this situation, you must rotate yourself so that by successive movements, you will squarely face all the areas or persons you're responsible for. Facing fully helps you size up a situation. You can see best when you are directly facing persons. When your goal is communication with persons (Section II), this also lets them know that you are open to hearing them.

Of course, if safety is an issue, then you would not face a person or situation that exposes you to physical harm or danger.

VIDEO **"Facing Squarely: The Wrong Way and the Right Way"**

Looking directly. When positioning yourself, you should look directly at the area or person(s) you are managing. Unless you look directly, you will not be on top of the situation, even if you are in the right position and are facing squarely. Looking directly at a group often involves looking at their eyes. When questioning a person, for example, you will be able to get important clues by closely observing their eyes and their facial expression.

In addition to gaining information, your direct look tells people that you are confident and are not threatened. This doesn't mean you get involved in a staring contest. But many people believe that a person who won't look you in the eyes is being deceptive.

POSITIONING means looking directly
at the area and person or persons
you are managing.

Eye contact may also be the best way of communicating interest. When a person sees you looking directly at their face, they become aware of your effort to make contact with them. In addition, looking directly at people will provide you with valuable information about them. People who keep shifting their eyes while talking to you signal that, at the very least, they are either uncomfortable with you or with what is being said. This kind of information is important in law enforcement.

You must also keep in mind that "direct" eye contact may be threatening to some people based on the individual or circumstances (e.g., cultural differences).

VIDEO **"Looking Directly: The Wrong Way and the Right Way"**

You probably have many duty stations (cubicle, office, roll-call room). Think of some of these stations. Describe where you would position yourself to size up the situation.

Station: _____

Position: _____

_____

Station: _____

Position: _____

_____

List two situations in which you think it would be a good idea to look a supervisee directly in the eye.

1) _____

2) _____

List two situations in which you think it would *not* be a good idea to look a supervisee directly in the eye.

1) _____

2) _____

ROLE-PLAY ACTIVITY

Supervisee	Supervisor	Group
Role plays for 20 seconds	Positions for 20 seconds • Distancing • Squaring • Looking directly	Critiques supervisor for appropriate-ness of his or her position

Posturing

Using good posture means holding your body in a way that shows strength, confidence, interest, and control. When you appear strong and confident, people will believe that you are strong and confident.

THE BASICS

Sizing Up the Situation

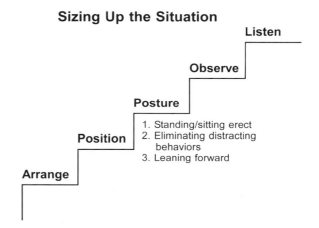

Posture
1. Standing/sitting erect
2. Eliminating distracting behaviors
3. Leaning forward

Your posture—how you carry yourself—tells people a lot. It can make a person think that you're confident of yourself or that you're really pretty worried about what might happen. Your aim, of course, should be to show your real confidence.

As with positioning, there are several ways in which you can use posturing when you are sizing up the situation. Here, we'll focus on three specific procedures: standing/sitting erect, eliminating distracting behaviors, and leaning forward.

The way in which the first two procedures show confidence should be obvious. When you stand or sit erect and get rid of distracting behaviors, you let people know that you're in full physical control—control, not only of your own body, but of the whole situation.

And that's essential! Many people will try to intimidate any supervisor who doesn't look as if he or she is confident about what he or she is doing. If a person thinks he or she can intimidate you, you're in real trouble. Any supervisor without respect is open to embarrassment and abuse.

Example For example, there was one supervisor who was known to avoid a situation at the first sign of trouble. Officers felt really uncomfortable with this person as a supervisor. But while most of the officers didn't trust this individual, other officers were always taking advantage and getting what they wanted.

Eventually, there were reports of officers on their shift sleeping while on duty, abusing citizens, and exhibiting slow response times. The final blow was a situation where a questionable shooting of a suspect put the whole department in a liability situation.

By standing erect and eliminating distracting habits, you show your strength and that you mean business. The third part of the posturing skills outlined here, leaning forward, can also show confidence by reinforcing the idea that you are committing all your attention and potential energy to job performance. But leaning forward, as you will see in Section II, can also help you communicate your interest when you choose to provide any human service. Used in this way, such a posture says to a person, "I am inclined to listen, to pay attention, to be interested, to help."

All right, let's take a closer look at the three parts of posturing already outlined.

Standing/sitting erect. We all know the importance of erect posture. You probably heard it as a child, and you definitely heard it if you were in the armed services: "Stand your full height," "Be proud, stand up straight," "Stick out that chest," "Pull in that gut."

Erect posture takes muscle tone and practice. Look in the mirror and check yourself out. Are your shoulders straight? Is your chest caved in? How do you feel? Ask someone else for his or her reaction. Which way does he or she experience you as stronger and more confident?

POSTURING means standing/sitting
erect to show strength and confidence.

**"Erect Posture—Sitting or Standing:
The Wrong Way and the Right Way"**

Eliminating distracting behaviors. A person who can't stand steady is seen as not at ease with themselves or others. Nail biting, foot-tapping, and other distracting behaviors do not communicate confidence and control. But standing stiff like a board doesn't communicate it either. You should not feel tension in your body after you have eliminated distracting behaviors.

POSTURING means eliminating
all distracting behaviors.

**"Eliminating Distracting Behaviors:
The Wrong Way and the Right Way"**

List some distracting behaviors that **other officers** sometimes show.

_____

_____

_____

_____

What are some distracting behaviors that **you** sometimes show?

_____

_____

_____

_____

PART 3 OF POSTURING   **Leaning forward.** Your intention here must be to communicate interest and concern by shifting your weight forward so that people become more aware of your inclination to communicate and supervise them with respect. This communicates "moving closer" without actually moving you much closer or making any physical contact. Since this position shows you to be more alert, it also gives you more control over the situation. Now, try leaning your weight away from another person. What do you experience? Probably a "laid-back" sort of remoteness. You're simply not as involved.

POSTURING means leaning forward
to show that your attention is
really focused.

VIDEO   **"Leaning Forward: The Wrong Way and the Right Way"**

15

ROLE-PLAY ACTIVITY

Supervisee	Supervisor	Group
1) Talks for 30 seconds	**1) Positions:** • Distancing • Squaring • Looking directly **Postures:** • Sitting erect • Eliminating distracting behaviors • Leaning forward	**1)** Observes supervisor's ability to maintain positioning and posturing behaviors for 30 to 60 seconds
2) Talks for 60 seconds	**2)** Repeats above	**2)** Repeats above

16

Observing

Observing is the ability to notice and understand individuals' and groups' appearances, behaviors, and environment. Careful observation of actions will tell you most of what you need to know about people, their feelings, and their difficulties.

The four steps in Observing are:

INTERVENTION
MODEL

THE BASICS

Sizing Up the Situation

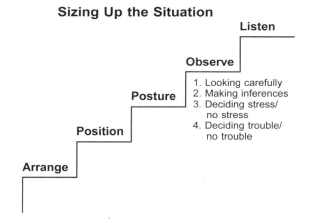

Listen

Observe
1. Looking carefully
2. Making inferences
3. Deciding stress/ no stress
4. Deciding trouble/ no trouble

Posture

Position

Arrange

PART 1 OF
OBSERVING **Looking carefully at behavior, appearance, and environment.** A *behavior* is a nonverbal cue provided by something that a person does while conscious and active. For example, you might observe any or all of the following behaviors: two people holding hands, one person bumping another, a person looking in a store window, a person wringing their hands.

An *appearance* is a nonverbal cue that a person might display even if he or she were unconscious or dead. For example, you might observe the following appearances: one

17

person is African-American, a second person didn't wear clean clothes today, a third person is an older person, a fourth person is wearing a T-shirt and shorts.

Environment is made up of the physical settings where people live and work—neighborhoods, homes, workplace—and the people they live with and relate to—friends, family, and co-workers. It also includes environmental experiences that have influenced their lives: education, military, vocation, and culture.

What is she doing?

How does she look?

Where is she? And with whom?

When observing a person, you should try to answer mental questions such as, "What's she doing right now?" (behavior), "What are the important things about how she looks?" (appearance), and "What's important about where she is and who she is with?" (environment). For example, a supervisee named Jim Barker has been coming to work late (behavior), his uniform is wrinkled and hair unkempt (appearance), he is separated from his wife and three children, and is living in an apartment alone (environment).

OBSERVING means looking at behavior, appearances, and environment.

Once you're able to answer these questions, you're ready to draw some inferences about a person.

VIDEO | **"Observing Behavior, Appearance, and Environment"**

18

Making inferences about feelings, relationships, energy level, and values. *Inferences* are the initial conclusions you come to as the result of observing people. You take in visual cues related to a person's appearance, behavior, and environment. These cues are really "clues" that show you something about a person's feelings, relationships, energy levels, and values. The more observations you make, the more inferences you can draw—and the more accurate these inferences will be. Inferences are important because they provide valuable information that increases your ability to manage another person or predict that person's future behavior. For example, Jim may be feeling "down" (feeling) due to his separation from his wife and children (relationship) and his poor grooming may be due to low motivation (energy) due to not seeing his children (values being a parent).

OBSERVING means making
inferences about feelings,
relationships, energy levels, and values.

**Making
inferences
about feelings**

**Is he positive,
negative, or
neutral about
others?**

The supervisor can use his or her observing skills to draw inferences about how an individual, or an entire group of people, is feeling. Knowing how a person is feeling is critical in determining where a person really is. For example, you might use the feeling word *happy* to describe a person who is exercising and smiling. For a person who is pacing while wringing his hands, you might apply the feeling word *tense.* You might use the term *uptight* to describe a group of persons who are tightly clustered and speaking with each other in a well-guarded, hesitant manner.

19

What feeling word would you apply to the following examples?

1) A supervisee is sitting on a bench in the locker room, head hanging down, clenching his fist and staring straight ahead.

Feeling Word: _____

2) Sitting at a desk, a supervisee is holding up a piece of letter-sized paper, while pointing to it and smiling broadly, laughing and occasionally waving the paper around.

Feeling Word: _____

VIDEO **"Inferring Feelings and Why"**

Making inferences about relationship

Besides being aware of the nonverbal cues that indicate the feelings of a person, a supervisor can further increase his or her effectiveness in management by looking for cues that indicate the nature of the relationship between themselves and the people he or she works with and supervises, and among people in general. The relationship between the supervisor and his or her supervisees, and people in general, serves as a good indicator of future action.

A supervisee who has a good relationship with you may take directives from you without difficulty or conflict. Conversely, one who has a poor relationship with you may be hard to motivate to follow your directives.

Is he positive, negative, or neutral about others?

In general, you can categorize relationships and feelings as positive, negative, or neutral. People who do things to make your job easier (e.g., keep you informed) probably have, or want to have, a positive relationship with you. A person who always tries to hassle you (e.g., uses abusive language, refuses to obey orders) doesn't have, or doesn't want to have, a positive relationship with you. When a relationship is a neutral relationship, it is purely business and has no emotional component, positive or negative (e.g., a business transaction in a store).

Example

Among people, relationships of power are critical. It's common for people to form their own group with a leader. Knowing the relationship within and between groups is crucial. For example, a group of officers working a certain zone go out together after work. One of the supervisees within the group has had a couple of run-ins with you, their supervisor. He is also the informal leader of the group. You begin to notice that some of the supervisees in his group are now acting differently toward you. This situation could obviously affect your ability to supervise these other individuals if you start to have a negative relationship with them.

21

List two behaviors and/or appearances that would tell you that two persons have a negative relationship:

1) *Keeps Their distance*

2) _____

What might result from these behaviors and/or appearances?

_____

_____

List two behaviors and/or appearances that would tell you that two persons have a positive relationship:

1) _____

2) _____

Energy: high?   low?   moderate?

_____

"Inferring Relationships and Why"

Making inferences about energy level Energy level tells us a great deal about how much and what type of trouble a person can or may cause. For example, persons with low energy levels are reluctant to initiate anything. They look and act defeated. Their movements are slow, their heads hang down, and every move seems like an effort. These individuals **Low?** may spend a good part of their time being non-productive. People with moderate energy **Moderate?** levels actively engage in most activities (e.g., playing, working, talking, eating) while high **High?** energy persons not only participate in all that is required but also make use of physical fit- ness programs and many other activities. The

22

danger of high energy, of course, is that this energy needs to be used constructively so that it does not become a source of problems.

While it is important to observe basic levels of energy, changes in energy level are even more critical. Energy levels are usually constant for people, except at special times (e.g., weekends, special sporting events, holidays). Abrupt changes from high to low to high may indicate trouble (to self or others).

PRACTICE

List two behaviors that show a high energy level:

1) _____

2) _____

List two behaviors that show a low energy level:

1) _____

2) _____

List two special times that might cause energy levels to change:

1) _____

2) _____

VIDEO **"Inferring Energy Level and Why"**

Making inferences about values

It is also important to understand as much as possible about a person's values. Here is where observing the environment comes in. Every person has three basic environments: the place where he or she lives, the place where he or she works, and the place where he or she learns. In each of these settings, the actual environment will include not only physical materials, but also people—the people a person "hangs with." You can learn a great deal about a person by carefully observing his or her environment. A general rule is this: What a person gives his or her energy to is of value to them; the more energy given, the higher the value.

What interests a person?

Values are the ideas (e.g., religious beliefs), things (e.g., automobiles, jewelry), and people (e.g., spouse, children) a person has a strong bond toward.

Knowing what a person values has real implications for effective supervisors. When you know what a person wants and doesn't want, you've got an edge in supervising that person when necessary.

PRACTICE

List three of *your* important values:

1) _____
2) _____
3) _____

VIDEO "Inferring Values and Why"

Reasons should be observable, concrete The reasons for your inferences should come from **visual cues** related to **behaviors, appearances,** and **environment.** Inferences stand the best chance of being accurate if they are based on detailed and concrete observations rather than on vague and general ones (e.g., black hair, scar on cheek, shaking their fist, with three other males in locker room).

PRACTICE Read the following incident carefully. Be ready to give reasons (i.e., descriptions of appearances and behaviors) for some inferences you will be asked to draw.

Incident **4:30 p.m. Shift Change.** You observe four supervisees in the locker room. You notice one is standing, addressing the other three who are sitting. He has no shirt on with only a towel wrapped around him. He is pointing his finger at one of the three. He has a scowl on his face. When the supervisee he is pointing at tries to speak and one of the other supervisees tries to say something, the standing supervisee looks directly at them and cuts them off.

Write down the feelings of the standing supervisee, his relationship to the group, and his energy level. Cite reasons for your inferences. **Note:** The reasons should be descriptions of the appearances and behaviors demonstrated that support your inferences.

Feelings (angry, scared, happy, sad):

_____

Reason: _____

_____

_____

Relationship to group (positive, negative, neutral): _____

Reason: _____

_____

_____

Energy Level (high, moderate, low):

_____

Reason: _____

_____

_____

PART 3 OF
OBSERVING

Deciding whether things are stressful or not stressful for a given person or persons. Once you've been on the job for some time, you get to know how individuals tend to function through observation. One person is easygoing and hardly ever hassles you or others. Another always looks like they're mad at the world. A third always seems to be engaged in self-pity. Your observations and the inferences you draw can help you determine whether a particular person is in a "stress" or "no stress" condition for him- or herself at any point in time.

OBSERVING means determining if things are stressful or not stressful.

In determining whether things are stressful or not stressful for a given person or group at a given time, compare your present observations with any past ones and/or with any comments that other officers may have made about these people. For example, you may observe an individual   arguing   loudly   with another person. He may even be making threats. If this is normal behavior for this person, you probably need to exercise only the usual amount of caution. But if the appearance and behavior of the angry person is highly unusual or abnormal for him, you'll know it's a potentially troublesome situation.

Example Normal behavior for Jim Barker, the individual mentioned previously (separated from his wife and three children), is smiling when you initially see him and being very animated (using his hands while talking). His normal appearance is to have his hair neatly combed, to be washed regularly, and to have his uniform pressed and creased perfectly, with shoes polished. Since his separation from his wife and children (environment) his behavior and appearance have changed (i.e., not smiling very much, not animated, and uniform and shoes not kept up).

VIDEO   **"Decide Stress or No Stress"**

PART 4 OF OBSERVING **Deciding if there is trouble or no trouble.** This decision should be based on your observations and your knowledge of the person or persons. As you gain more knowledge about a person, you will be able to generate information that will be useful in making this decision despite "abrupt and/or major changes in behavior and/or appearance that could mean trouble."

OBSERVING means deciding whether it's a "trouble" or "no trouble" situation.

"Decide Trouble or No Trouble"

CONCLUSION

Important to know

Observing appearance and behavior is usually the quickest and most accurate way to detect whether or not a given individual is really having a problem. People may be very reluctant to talk to you about problems. Your observations will allow you to anticipate problems so that you can prepare for their possible impact on other people, you, other officers, or the persons themselves. **Remember, nonverbal behavior accounts for 65 to 90 percent of any spoken message.**

PRACTICE

Your instructor will guide the group through role-playing activities that will give you more practice in using the skill of Observing.

1) Feeling: _____

   Reason: _____

   _____

2) Relationship: _____

   Reason: _____

   _____

3) Energy Level: _____

   Reason: _____

   _____

4) What knowledge or principles do you have that would apply to the situation?

_____

_____

_____

_____

5) Stress or no stress? _____

6) Trouble or no trouble? _____

ROLE-PLAY ACTIVITY

Supervisee	Supervisor	Group
1) Describes setting	**1)** Positions Postures	**1)** Pays attention
2) Role plays for 60 seconds (tells story about where he/she grew up)	**2)** Observes behavior appearance	**2)** Writes own answers to behavior, appearance, feelings, relationship, energy level, value, mood of supervisee
3) Provides nonverbal cues (behaviors) while conveying story	**3)** Infers feelings, relationship, energy level, values	
	4) Describes mood	

Listening

Listening is the ability to hear and understand what people are really saying. Listening helps you hear the signals from people while things are still at the verbal stage so that you can take appropriate action to manage situations before they get out of hand.

INTERVENTION MODEL

THE BASICS

Sizing Up the Situation

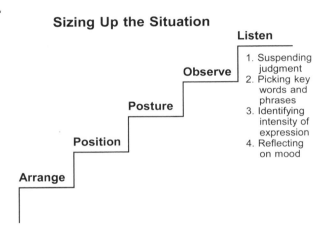

Listen

1. Suspending judgment
2. Picking key words and phrases
3. Identifying intensity of expression
4. Reflecting on mood

Observe

Posture

Position

Arrange

VERBAL CUES AND SIGNALS

People often go through a verbal stage before the action begins. If you can hear the signals, you can cut off the trouble before it really breaks out. Listening involves your ability to hear and accurately recall all the important verbal cues used by people—"important" because of implied signals of trouble or problems. The danger may be an individual's intention to get into trouble, harm another person, etc.

Complaints are common, of course, but they're also important. An effective supervisor listens to complaints and recognizes when a familiar cue is uttered in a new tone—or when a complaint arises from a normal, uncomplaining person. A supervisor listens especially for changes: silence when there is usually noise or noise when there is usually silence. Once again, the supervisor asks the question: "Is there trouble here?"

GETTING READY TO LISTEN

As indicated, you should get ready for listening by using the basic arranging, positioning, posturing, and observing skills whenever possible.

Arrange

Arranging your environment to eliminate distractions and to make it pleasant will help you focus on the person talking.

Position

A good position will obviously help you hear better.

Posture

Posturing, while perhaps less important in terms of listening for good management, is essential when you're listening to a person who really wants to talk to you. Your posture can signal to the person that you're focusing all your attention on them.

Observe

Finally, your observing skills cannot always be used to promote better listening— for example, you may overhear something that people are talking about around the corner. But when possible, visual observations help you understand the implications of what you're hearing. A person who sounds angry but turns out to be leaning back in his chair and grinning may have only been telling a story to others; an individual whose angry voice fits with his tense, uptight appearance presents quite a different situation.

One more preliminary thing: you can't listen effectively to people if you've got other things on your mind. If you're thinking about home or other job responsibilities, you may miss a lot of what is said and what it really

31

means. You've got to focus on the person to whom you're listening—and this takes a good deal of concentration. You can work to develop this kind of concentration by reviewing what you're going to do and who you're going to see before you begin work. Then you'll really be ready to start using the four specific procedures that skilled listening involves.

PART 1 OF
LISTENING **Suspending judgment.** This is very difficult to do for anyone and especially for those in law enforcement. In many circumstances, you have just witnessed a violation of the law. If, however, your goal is to get more information, you will need to get people to open up more. Suspending judgment, at least temporarily, can assist with that.

It is still hard at times to listen without immediately judging because many people with whom you must deal get defensive (e.g., clam up, get upset, or become vague) very quickly when you, as a law enforcement officer, try to talk with them. Despite this, it will severely hurt your management efforts if you do not suspend judgment because you will never hear the real verbal cues you need to get more information or to assist someone.

LISTENING means **suspending your own judgment** temporarily so that you can really hear what is being said.

All complaints sound the same after a while—but they are not all the same! Some are just the normal whines and gripes, while others are real warning signals of potential problems. Just let the message sink in before making any decisions about it. Of course, certain situations call for quick action, but if you develop your nonjudgmental listening ability, you will hear better and be able to take appropriate action more quickly when necessary.

VIDEO

"Suspending Judgment: The Wrong Way and the Right Way"

PART 2 OF LISTENING

Picking out key words and phrases. There are key words and phrases to listen for. Here are a few: *kill, depressed, snitch, honky, waste, hawk, staff.* Of course, everything you hear and see must be considered in terms of who did or said it; some people are always sounding off. In addition to the key words you hear, it's important to add your observations and knowledge of the person who said them.

LISTENING means **picking out the key words/phrases** such as *snitch* or *kiss-up.*

PRACTICE

List some words and phrases that signal danger or trouble in your particular environment.

Example

On the take _____   Vice operation _____

_____   _____

_____   _____

VIDEO

"Pick Out Key Words and Phrases: The Wrong Way and the Right Way"

33

Volume?
Emotion?
Intensity?
High,
moderate,
low?

Identifying intensity of expression. Statements are made with varying intensity (high, moderate, and low). The louder and more emotional a statement, the more intense it is. But loudness and emotion are not the same thing. A wavering voice, for example, signals a lot of emotion even though it may not be loud. A statement that is either loud or emotional but not both is most often of moderate intensity.

A statement that is loud and is empty of emotion is usually of low intensity. High intensity statements are very real signs of danger.

VIDEO **"Identify Intensity of Expression: High, Moderate, or Low"**

LISTENING means **determining whether the intensity of a person's speech is high, moderate, or low.**

Reflecting on what the mood is. Is the person's mood positive, negative, neutral? Normal or abnormal? Why? *Mood* here means, at a very simple level, what people are feeling. One question you might ask to determine mood is "What kinds of feelings are being expressed or implied (positive, negative, or neutral)?"

Another question you want to answer is, "Is this mood normal or abnormal for this time and place?" Sure, there are always exceptions. For example, a man can say, "I'm going to kill you," quietly and without emotion, yet still mean it. This is why it is so important to know as much as possible and to continue to observe and listen for other cues.

LISTENING means **determining whether a mood is positive, neutral, or negative,** and whether this mood is **normal or abnormal.**

Reasons   When you answer the question, "Is this normal or abnormal?" you should try to formulate the reason why this is the case. "Normal" means "as it usually is." This can apply to one person as well as to a large group of persons. People are usually quite consistent in their behaviors in their various settings. As we say, "they are creatures of habit." For example, it's not normal for people to be really quiet when they are among others who are being very noisy and animated.

VIDEO   **"Identify Mood: Positive, Negative, or Neutral"**

ROLE-PLAY ACTIVITY	Supervisee	Supervisor	Group
	1) Describes setting	**1)** Positions Postures Observes Suspends judgment Says nothing	**1)** Positions for paying attention
	2) Role plays person for 20 to 30 seconds		**2)** Writes own answers
	3) Provides verbal cues for conveying information (high, moderate, low)	**2)** Pulls out key words	**3)** Rates supervisor on sizing-up skills
	4) Defines mood (positive, negative, neutral)	**3)** Identifies intensity	
	5) Identifies mood as normal or abnormal	**4)** Rates supervisee on #2 through #6 (Yes/No)	
	6) Why?		

Summary of the Basics

You are a field training officer (FTO) working with a rookie. You're trying to teach this rookie the ins and outs of using basic skills while working in a park. You see the following: On one bench, two older fellows are talking softly—their usual behavior. You've watched them before. They'd talk for an hour—no more, no less—all part of their own little routine. No problems. Another place, a young guy is laying on his back in a grassy area, and an older man paces back and forth near him. Tension there: one guy lying quietly, another appearing pretty nervous.

"How's it going?" You stop three or four feet from the older man who had turned so that you could face him squarely, and at the same time, you could easily observe the younger guy on the ground. "Is that your buddy there on the grass?"

The older man nodded and said, "Yeah, he's not feeling so good, so he's getting a snooze in." He then went back to pacing. You turn slightly to get closer to the young guy. Since the older guy still seems nervous, you position yourself so that you can keep him in view while you size up the younger man.

Upon closer observation, you notice saliva oozing from the corner of the younger guy's mouth. His lips appear bluish and you notice that his respiration appears shallow and erratic. You immediately put in a call for backup and for an emergency medical response. This guy isn't snoozing, he's not functioning normally.

All right, you've had a chance to learn the five basic skills you need to size up a situation—to manage your job and people more effectively. You've practiced arranging, positioning, posturing, observing, and listening. But as you know, there's far more to being an effective officer than being able to size things up. There will be times when you choose to manage by communicating. You'll want to defuse a troublesome situation or get important information. There may even be times you choose to become more involved.

In the second major section of this manual, we'll consider the skills you'll need to communicate effectively. The skills in this section, while often secondary to other management skills in some situations, are absolutely essential when dealing with many tense situations—situations where strong feelings may get out of control or are interfering with your ability to understand what you need to. Sizing things up just lets you know what's happening and what may happen. To manage things for the better—and that's what effective management requires—you need to add on communication skills!

THE ADD-ONS

1. Respond
2. Ask Questions

THE BASICS

1. Arrange
2. Position
3. Posture
4. Listen
5. Observe

Section II

The Add-Ons:
Communicating with People

Add-on skills help you open up communication with people. They provide you with the ability to get another person to tell you more about what he or she knows or thinks. You'll find the add-on communicating skills invaluable whenever you need to get more information about a situation, or when you **choose** to become involved.

The two add-on communicating skills are:

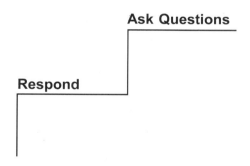

THE ADD-ONS

Communicating with People

Ask Questions

Respond

It's been said that the only thing worse than a young person who thinks they know it all is an older person who's sure they know it all—but doesn't. Some of you will be new to supervision while others will have varying degrees of experience. Whatever your situation, you've probably run across supervisors who are very rigid in their approach. They see little need for juries or judges. To these supervisors, anything less than "throwing the book" is weak and the reason the system doesn't work. There's a lot of logic in their thinking, but only up to a point.

Example   One supervisor found this out to his considerable embarrassment. A new officer recently started work and was cheerful enough, but didn't say much. But then again, what would a man with only a few months' experience have to say anyway? Even so, the experienced supervisor figured him for an academy whiz kid who thought he had all the answers. He didn't.

One day the two happened to be on duty together. A street character named Larry took the supervisor aside and tipped him off about some drugs that Jess, another transient, had stashed. Minutes later, the experienced officer had Jess and was conducting a thorough search of the "room" he slept in. Sure enough, they found a small amount of drugs hidden in his bedding.

"That's kind of hard to believe," the young officer said to the supervisor once Jess had been written up.

"Yea? Why's that?"

"Well, I've seen Jess around—and I've watched who he hangs out with. He doesn't seem like the kind of guy who's into drugs."

The supervisor shrugged. "Who knows? All that counts is that we found this in his bed. He can try to deny that it's his, but there's no getting around the facts."

Jess did deny it. He swore that he knew nothing about the "stuff." The officer, recognizing that they had the guy "cold," decided to open Jess up, since he was so persistent in his innocence:

40

Officer: You seem awfully upset about this situation.

Jess: You bet I am! These guys have been trying to get me to push this stuff for months and when I refused, they decided to set me up to teach me a lesson!

Officer: So you're saying that they set you up because you wouldn't go along.

Jess: That's it. It's no alibi. If you check it out with some of the other street people they'll back me up.

Officer: Who could I talk with who might know?

Jess: Artie, the guy who cleans up at the Mexican joint over on Palmer Street, could run it down to you. Be cool though, and don't put him on Front Street.

Officer: So, this Artie could give us some information?

Jess: Right!

Officer: OK. I'll check this all out. In the meantime, though, I'll have to book you until we see how it all washes out.

Skills make the difference Well it did "wash out"; Jess was telling the truth and it was verified. Larry was picked up and eventually provided the officers with useful information about some of the transactions on the street and was able to name some names.

41

The use of skills here really had a payoff. But just what is communication all about? We know that some officers can really talk with people and others can't.

Why it's important to communicate

Although you see and hear all the time, chances are you're never really sure what's really going on inside another person. At the most fundamental level, people are all human beings and probably much more alike than different, even though it's obvious that criminals are not the same as law enforcement officers. The gulf between you and other people may often be frustrating. In one way you feel that you know a person, but in another way, you're sure you don't. And knowing other people is important at times. The better your understanding of another person, the more effective you can be in terms of managing him or her.

Understanding means effectiveness

Communication promotes understanding

This is where communication skills become important add-ons. When you choose to use these skills, you can find out a great deal more about where individuals are coming from. You can add to your understanding and action in ways that will help you defuse tension, decrease the chances of trouble, and increase your ability to handle any and all situations more effectively. The basic skills covered in Section I let you size up the situation. The add-on communication skills presented in this section let you understand the full implications of that situation and act constructively.

WHAT ARE THE SKILLS? Once you choose to communicate, you begin by putting all of the five basic skills to use: arranging, positioning, posturing, observing, and listening. As the process of communicating develops, you use new skills in two important ways.

The two skills
- Responding to people
- Asking relevant questions

As the materials that follow make clear, responding to people means a good deal more than just answering a greeting—although this, too, can be important. You need to take the initiative in developing effective responses. By the same token, asking relevant questions means more than a simple, "Hey, what's going on?" Here, in Section II, you'll have a chance to learn the specific procedures involved in responding and asking questions effectively.

GET READY BY USING THE BASICS As noted, communicating must begin with your use of all the basic skills. You arrange your environment to eliminate distractions and make it pleasant. You position yourself at the best possible distance—say three to four feet when you are talking with a single person (although this would certainly increase if you sized up danger). This puts you close enough to see and hear everything, yet not so close that you seem overly threatening. You face the individual squarely, your left shoulder squared with his or her right and your right with his or her left. And you look directly at the person, making appropriate eye contact to let him or her know you are really "right there."

43

You position yourself to communicate both confidence and real attention. You observe the appearance, behavior, and environment, using visual cues to draw inferences about feelings, the relationship with you, and the general energy level. You listen carefully, making sure you take in all the key words and verbal indications of intensity so that you can determine just what a person's need really is. Only after you have really mastered and put to use the basic skills will you be able to use the add-on communication skills effectively.

Like the basic skills, communication skills involve a step-by-step approach. First you respond to the person. Then you ask any relevant questions you need to ask. Then you respond again, this time to the answers. You would usually not, in other words, just jump in and start asking questions—at least, not if your goal is to get the person to open up and communicate useful information voluntarily. There may be times when the circumstances warrant using more intimidating tactics. However, we do not have to teach intimidation, and intimidation always contains significant risk.

PRACTICE We have all met supervisors who are better at communicating than other supervisors. What qualities or skills did these good communicators have that made them effective? List two.

1) _____

_____

2) _____

_____

Responding

Responding means just that—showing a clear reaction to something that you have seen or heard. A response **gives evidence** that you have listened. In this section, we'll take a look at several levels of responding. At the simplest level, you can respond to content by summarizing and expressing what a person or group of persons has said or done. At the next level, you can respond to the feelings shown in a person's words or reflected in his actions, particular feelings, and the reasons for those feelings.

There are three levels of responding:

INTERVENTION
MODEL

THE ADD-ONS

Communicating with People

Ask Questions

Respond

1. Responding to content
2. Responding to feeling
3. Responding to feeling
   and meaning

Each new level of responding does more to show a person that you really are on top of things—seeing, hearing, and understanding him in terms of where he is. Probably more than anything else in this training, the concept of responding is going to seem strange to you. It's new and you may be doubtful about its worth. There are some things to remember here:

1) We are not telling you that you can't use other communications techniques that have worked for you in the past.

2) We are trying to "add-on" to techniques you may already have to increase your communication abilities.

3) The more techniques you have to handle a given situation in life, the greater your chances of success or control of the outcome.

Responding to content. Responding to content is the skill of seeing and hearing what is really happening and the ability to reflect that understanding back to a person. When you respond to content, you are letting a person know that you heard him or her accurately and are on top of the situation.

While your use of the basic skills establishes a relationship in which people are more likely to cooperate with and talk to you, responding is a tool you can use spontaneously to communicate with anyone. Responding to content is the first part of effective responding. It shows a person that you have heard or seen what he or she said or did. When any person, including someone you must supervise, knows that you are seeing and/or hearing them accurately, he or she will tend to talk more freely. This is critical because talking not only gives you more of the information you need, it also allows people to get things off their chest.

There are two steps to responding to content: a) reflecting on what was said and b) using the responding format to respond to content.

46

Ask Questions

Respond

1. Responding to content:
   a) Reflect on what was seen and heard
   b) Use responding format to respond to content

Use the basics

When responding to content, you are focused on what people are either saying or doing. Using what you have learned, you focus by posturing and positioning yourself for observing and/or listening to the person.

Reflect on what was seen and heard

Next, you reflect on what you have seen and heard: "What is he doing?" "What is he saying?" "How does he look?" In answering these questions, stick close to what is actually going on and/or what is being said.

Use responding format

Finally, after taking it all in and reflecting on it, you summarize, in your own words, what the person is saying or doing. You respond to the content by saying to a person either:

"You look (it looks) _____" or
"You're saying _____."

(For example, "You look pretty busy" or "You're saying you're pretty busy.")

You respond to content when you want more information to aid you in management. This may occur when you are interrogating or when you notice unusual behavior in a person or group of persons and would like to get some information from them about what they are doing. For example, you might notice a group of unusually talkative officers being very quiet. You could say to them: "You are all pretty quiet today." This gives them the opportunity to respond to you while also letting them know that you are observing them and observing them accurately. Unlike other approaches designed to get information, responding to content doesn't automatically put people on the defensive.

RESPONDING at the simplest
level reflects content:

"You're saying _____."

PRACTICE List two examples of situations in which you might respond to content in order to get more information from a supervisee.

1) _____

2) _____

List two reasons why you might want to get involved with a supervisee.

1) _____

2) _____

Example Here's an example. You are in your office talking with two officers, a male officer and a female officer, who aren't getting along. You "position" yourself out from behind your desk and place their chairs so that you are facing them squarely and can look directly at them at an appropriate distance. You "posture" yourself so that they know they have your full attention.

48

You instruct the officers on your ground rules: Only one person talks at a time. The female officer speaks, "He is always telling me he'll handle situations that he believes I'm not capable of because I'm a female. He tells me, based on his experience, females can't handle certain situations without messing them up."

You respond, "So you're telling me he's not letting you handle situations he believes should not be handled by females based on his experience." She says, "That's right."

You ask the male officer to tell you his side. "Well, I had this other female partner and there were situations I didn't think she should take the lead on, and she had no problem with that."

You respond, "So you believe that based on your prior experience with a female partner, you know what's best for your new female partner." The male officer says, "You got it."

VIDEO **"Responding to Content: The Wrong Way and the Right Way"**

ROLE-PLAY ACTIVITY	Supervisee	Supervisor	Group
	1) Gives the setting **2)** Role plays	**1)** Positions Postures Observes Listens **2)** Waits 30 seconds **3)** Gives responses: "You're saying _____." "You look (it looks) _____."	**1)** Positions Postures Observes Listens **2)** Writes own responses **3)** Rates supervisor's response: "Yes" if accurate, "No" if not, plus reason

Get people to talk instead of act

A typical emotion experienced by supervisees when they encounter supervisors can be anxiety. Of course, if you are the supervisee who has summoned the supervisor for assistance, the typical impact upon observing the responding supervisor will be a reduction of your anxiety. On the other hand, if you think you have done something wrong or you are going to be critiqued by a supervisor, your anxiety is likely to increase.

When supervising people who have anxiety, it's a good idea to let people talk off some of their anxiety rather than for them to act it out. Responding will assist greatly in accomplishing this.

You observe the female officer's facial expression. Inferring that she's angry, you say, "You look (inference) annoyed." She responds, "I am annoyed because I know what I'm doing."

You are now setting the stage for the next responding skill: responding to feeling.

50

Responding to feeling. Responding to feeling is the ability to capture in words the specific feeling experience being presented by a person. By responding to, or reflecting back, the person's feeling, you show that you understand that feeling. This encourages the person to talk and to release his or her feelings.

The two steps to responding to feeling are: a) reflect on feeling and b) reflect on feeling and intensity.

Ask Questions

Respond

1. Responding to content
2. Responding to feeling:
    a) Reflect on feeling
    b) Reflect on feeling
       and intensity

Every supervisee has feelings that affect what he or she says and does. The nature and strength of these feelings usually determine what a supervisee is going to do. When you respond to a supervisee's feelings, you are encouraging him or her to talk. The skill of responding to feelings has important implications for the management of supervisees.

RESPONDING at the next level
reflects feelings:

"You feel _____."

51

Understanding can defuse bad feelings! Showing that you understand how a supervisee feels can be more powerful than showing that you understand the content of their actions and/or words. Showing a supervisee that you understand their negative feelings can usually **defuse** those negative feelings. By responding to feelings at the verbal or "symbolic" behavior level, you keep the person's words from turning to action. Also, responding to feelings at a verbal level can give you the necessary clues to determine the supervisee's intention. If they clam up after you have responded to their feelings, they may be telling you that they are going to act on them; on the other hand, if they go with it verbally, they are telling you that they want to talk it out instead of acting on it. We all know the difference between a talking fight, where the parties are looking for a way out ("Yeah" versus "Oh, yeah!"), and a real fight where the fists are flying.

Greater understanding Besides being able to defuse negative feelings so that words don't become negative actions, responding to feelings leads to greater understanding of a supervisee. A supervisee can't always link up his or her feelings to the situation and is often at a loss as to where he or she is. In addition, when you respond to positive feelings, these feelings get reinforced (unlike negative feelings). There's nothing mysterious about this. We don't enjoy our negative feelings, so we get rid of them by sharing them—by "talking them out." But we do enjoy our positive feelings, so they only become stronger when they're shared with another person. You can choose to strengthen the positive feelings that will help a supervisee act more positively simply by recognizing and responding to these feelings. As a general rule, a person who feels positive about him- or herself will try to do positive things, while a person who feels negative about him- or herself will try to do negative things. If you push this out, you arrive at the general principle: **People tend to act in ways consistent with the way other significant people see and act toward them.**

PRACTICE

List two situations where it would be important and useful to defuse negative feelings of a supervisee.

1) _____

_____

2) _____

_____

Use the basics

For responding to feeling, you arrange your environment, position and posture yourself, then observe and listen. Then you reflect for the feeling (happy, angry, sad, scared) and its intensity (high, medium, or low).

Finally, you respond by saying:

"You feel _____ ."

(For example, "You feel angry.")

Reflecting on feeling

Here, the new skill involves reflecting for feeling and intensity. Adding a new skill doesn't mean discarding the old skills, of course. When reflecting for feeling, you are really asking yourself, "Given what I see and hear, how does this supervisee basically

53

Happy?
Angry?
Sad?
Scared?
Confused?

feel?" Are they happy, angry, sad, scared, or confused? This supervisee's behavior and words will let you make a good guess at the feeling. For example, a supervisee who shouts at another person, "You stupid idiot, now look what you've done!" while shaking her fist and getting red in the face is obviously feeling a level of anger.

Reflect on intensity of feelings

High?
Medium?
Low?

After you have picked out the feeling word, you must reflect on the intensity of the feeling. For example, anger can be high in intensity (boiling mad), medium in intensity (frustrated), or low in intensity (concern). The more accurate your feeling word reflects the intensity, the more effective your response will be. That is, your response will be more accurate and will do the job better (i.e., defuse the negative feeling). You wouldn't choose "concerned" for the above example because the term is too weak to describe a woman yelling, shaking her fist, and turning red. Such an observation would probably only make them more angry. But, "You feel furious" would fit fine.

PRACTICE

Take each of the five basic feeling words (happy, angry, sad, scared, and confused) and write a high, medium, and low intensity word for each.

FEELING WORDS

	High	Medium	Low
Happy	_____	_____	_____
Angry	_____	_____	_____
Sad	_____	_____	_____
Scared	_____	_____	_____
Confused	_____	_____	_____

54

Below are some ground rules you should consider before the role-play activity:

1) People may not want to take responsibility for their emotions and deny they feel anything (don't pressure them).

2) People may correct you by expressing a feeling word that better describes how they feel (just let them).

3) The intensity of a person's feelings may be so high that they can't talk about them (so be patient, and go back to your basic skills: arrange, position, posture, observe, listen).

ROLE-PLAY ACTIVITY

Supervisee	Supervisor	Group
1) Shares real problem* **2)** Rates response after group training	**1)** Positions Postures Observes Listens **2)** Pauses 10 to 20 seconds **3)** Gives response: "You feel ___."	**1)** Positions Postures Observes Listens **2)** Writes own response: "You feel ___." **3)** Rates "Yes/No" on supervisor's response and tells why **4)** Gives individual response to group

Should not be anything that would be intimidating, embarrassing, or hurtful to self or others.

55

Responding to feeling and meaning.
Responding to feeling and meaning combines
the two previous skills. Responding to feeling
and meaning requires you to paraphrase the
content of a supervisee's statement in such a
way as to provide a meaningful reason for the
person's feeling.

The two steps in responding to feeling
and meaning are: a) reflect on the feeling and
the reason for that feeling, and b) respond to
the feeling and meaning.

Ask Questions

Respond

1. Responding to content
2. Responding to feeling
3. Responding to feeling and meaning
   a) Reflect on feeling and reason
   b) Respond to feeling and meaning

**Reflect on
feeling and
reason**

Learning how to respond to content and how
to respond to feeling has prepared you to
respond to feeling and meaning. Now, your
response at this new level can put everything
together. Here, you will capture effectively
where the person "is" at the moment. By adding the meaning to the feeling, you will help
yourself and the supervisee understand the
reason for their feelings about the situation.
The reason is simply the personal meaning
for the supervisee about what is happening.
For example, an officer in danger of being
pulled into a fight when his record is clean
and his promotion is coming up might feel
afraid because the fight could blow his

chances to get promoted. The personal meaning of the potential fight for this officer is that it might blow his chances. That is one reason why he hesitates, not because he's scared of fighting, but rather of not getting the promotion.

RESPONDING at the highest
level reflects both feeling
and meaning.

"You feel _____ because _____."

By putting together the feeling and meaning and then responding to both, you show a supervisee that you understand his or her experience as he or she presents it. This increases the chances that the supervisee will open up and talk even more to you. Additionally, you will be able to learn more about what the supervisee values and what bothers him or her so that you can gain a better understanding of him or her. This may be important in future conversations when you are helping a supervisee grow in their role and/or position (e.g., taking responsibility for problematic behavior).

Example **Officer:** Look, that person had it coming. I don't have to take that kind of crap from anybody.

Supervisor: You feel angry at me because you don't understand why this is necessary. In a situation like this, we just can't take chances; it's our procedure.

57

Officer: Well, it's embarrassing; it's like I'm a damn criminal.

Supervisor: I'm sorry about that, but it just has to be done.

The supervisor is responsive to the officer because he chooses to be. He believes it will—in both the short and long term—have a better impact. Note that he does this while continuing to carry out his duty. He keeps the intensity manageable by speaking calmly to the supervisee and acknowledging the supervisee's feelings and reasons for feeling that way—without necessarily agreeing or disagreeing with the supervisee.

In another situation, a citizen discusses a concern he has about his teenage son:

Citizen: He's headed for trouble. I just can't control him any more. All he listens to are the punks he runs with.

Supervising Officer: You feel worried because you know that, unless your son wakes up, he's going to be just like them.

Citizen: Yeah. They are into dope and none of them work. You know what's going to happen when you see that.

Supervising Officer: You feel kinda scared because you can see how the dope problem leads to other problems for kids.

58

Citizen:	Right, and it's getting worse, all the time, and I don't know what to do.
Supervising Officer:	Is he in school?
Citizen:	Yeah, he goes to the vo-tech school downtown.

The supervising officer understands clearly where the citizen is in the situation, where he wants (or needs) to be, and is able to suggest a possible solution. This became possible because he was able to attach an understanding of meaning to the feelings of the citizen.

Respond to feeling and meaning

By building on what you know, you add the reason to the feeling response you have just learned. Your new way of responding becomes "You feel _____ because _____."

What we need to focus on here, of course, is an individual's reason (i.e., personal meaning) for their feeling. Supplying the reason means that you must understand why what happened is important. You do this by rephrasing the content in your own words to capture that importance. You are actually giving the reason for the feeling. In this way, you make the person's feeling clearer and more understandable.

It is also important to capture whether the person is seeing him- or herself as responsible or seeing someone else as responsible. Your response should reflect where he sees the responsibility in the beginning, even though you may not agree. By doing this, you will have a better chance of getting the person to open up. You can always disagree when it becomes necessary and effective to do so. Remember, if you have this skill, you can choose to use it.

PRACTICE An officer is having problems at home in her marriage. Her job performance has suffered because of these personal problems. She says to you out of frustration:

"You know this job takes its toll on police marriages, and no one in this organization cares."

Identify the intensity and category of this feeling and pick an accurate feeling word to describe the person's emotion.

Feeling Word: _____

Now supply the reason for the officer's feeling. What does her situation really mean to her? Who is she blaming? Why is all of this so important to her? What does this mean to her? Put yourself in her place. Recognizing the meaning, formulate a response.

Response to Feeling and Meaning:

"You feel _____ because _____
_____ ."

The supervisor who was actually involved knew how to initiate communication with this officer in a tense situation like this—and he recognized that failure to do so could mean trouble. He knew that the person's basic feeling was upset. He knew that the intensity of this feeling was high, and that the person was really furious. And he knew that the officer was blaming the organization's demands for her marital problems, whether it was true or not—this was the meaning of the situation for the officer.

Knowing all of this, the supervisor was able to respond effectively to the feeling and to what this feeling meant: "You feel upset because you believe that this organization doesn't care how it affects an officer's marriage." This response caught the officer flat-footed. She had expected the supervisor to deny everything—to tell her to grow up and ignore the whole thing. She certainly hadn't expected the supervisor to respond to her situation at the same level that she was experiencing it!

Because the supervisor knew how to respond at this level, he was able to keep the officer talking openly. And in a tense situation, that can mean the difference between an effective supervisor and an ineffective supervisor.

Referral When responding to feeling and meaning, a communication interchange may sometimes go deeper than you feel you can handle. If this happens, you must consider the option of a referral. With your added understanding, your referral will be that much more specific and beneficial.

But many times, your added understanding will provide you with the information you need to really manage people. The payoff for you will be rewarding. Many officers put in their time, but don't get the payoff because they lack some of the skills needed to finish off the good start that they make by being decent and fair. Responding is one way to ensure the payoff.

Practice your responding skills with supervisors with whom you have been communicating. When you practice the skill, don't just give one response and say to yourself, "Well, I did it." Keep using your responding skills over and over again when you choose to understand. When you feel they have said all they are going to say, or when you know all you need to know, then you can take action.

But be careful about giving advice or getting involved. A lot of times a person will hold back until they see how you react. If you tell them what to do or become overly involved, you may be placing yourself in either a vulnerable situation or one over your head.

VIDEO **"Respond to Feeling and Meaning: The Wrong Way and the Right Way"**

ROLE-PLAY ACTIVITY	Supervisee	Supervisor	Group
	1) Gives real stimulus	**1)** Positions Postures Observes Listens	**1)** Positions Postures Observes Listens
	2) Gives spontaneous reply following each response	**2)** Pauses 10 to 20 seconds	**2)** Writes own response to feeling and meaning
	3) Rates responder after group rating	**3)** Gives response: "You feel _____."	**3)** Rates "Yes/No" on last response and tell why
		4) Pauses 10 to 20 seconds	**4)** Gives individual response to group
		5) Gives response: "You feel _____ because _____."	**5)** Gives feedback on responding to feeling and meaning

63

Asking Questions

You ask questions in order to get useful answers. Some questions get better answers than others: the skill of asking questions will help you increase your information base and hence your ability to manage others.

The two steps in asking questions are:

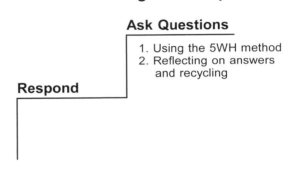

INTERVENTION MODEL

THE ADD-ONS

Communicating with People

Ask Questions

1. Using the 5WH method
2. Reflecting on answers and recycling

Respond

TWO STEPS IN ASKING QUESTIONS

As the following materials make clear, there are really two basic steps involved in asking relevant questions in an effective way. First, having responded to a person at the most accurate level, you must develop one or more **questions of the "5WH" type:** Who, What, Where, When, Why, and How. And second, you must **reflect** upon the answer or answers given by the person to make sure you fully understand all the implications. Did you get the information you wanted? Was new information revealed?

Asking questions will help you manage. If a person answered your questions satisfactorily, we would be all set. After all, we have all the right questions. The reality, however, is that for a variety of reasons (e.g., lack of trust, guilt), many people do not answer questions fully or accurately. In fact, questions will sometimes have the opposite effect—they will shut off communication with people rather than open it up. This is because questions are often seen as the bullets of the enemy ("Cover up, here they come"). The only way questions can be really effective in opening up a person is when they are used *in addition to* the basic skills plus responding. Use of the basics plus responding can get a person to the point where they will talk quite openly. It is then that questions can make their contribution by getting some of the necessary specifics (i.e., who, what, when, where, why, and how—the 5WH system).

Use the basics plus responding

PART 1 OF ASKING QUESTIONS **Asking 5WH questions.** Answers to questions will give you the detail you need to manage people effectively. The more details you know, the better you can understand what is going on. You always want to know **who** is involved, **what** they are doing or going to do, **when** and **where** something happened or will happen, **why** it did or will take place, and **how** it is going to be done or how it was done.

> "Where were you?"
> "Who were you with?"
> "Why were you there?"
> "What did you actually do?"
> "When did all this happen?"
> "How was it handled?"

Respond, then ask When you have all this information, you can take appropriate action and/or prevent problems from happening, now and maybe in the future. "Question asking" can be used with

65

responding during an interrogation, interview, or when you choose to assist with a problem.

Responding opens up the person and gives you a chance to make sure you understand what is being said. It also builds up trust with a person. For these reasons, you should always try to respond to a supervisee's actions or words at the highest possible level before you actually start asking questions. Questions then fill in the details of the picture. Often, details or reasons come from responding skills alone if you have patience. If the details do not surface, questions are appropriate; it's as simple as that.

PRACTICE For each of the following situations, first make a response and then ask appropriate questions.

1) You have an officer who has his second accident in two months in a police vehicle. He knows that his accident is largely due to his driving too fast in poor road conditions. You ask him to tell you what happened and the officer says:

"Sarge, I know this is my second wreck in two months, but honestly it wasn't my fault. This other car just cut in front of me unexpectedly and I couldn't stop."

Respond: "You feel _____

because _____

_____."

Questions (5WH):

_____

_____

2) An officer says to you: "I know the citizen said I was rude and cussed at her, but you needed to be there to get the full picture before you judge my actions."

Respond: "You feel _____

because _____."

Questions (5WH): _____

_____

_____

PART 2 OF ASKING QUESTIONS

Reflecting on answers to questions. It's not enough just to ask good questions. You also have to be able to make sense out of the answers you get while also recognizing, perhaps, the answers you're still not getting. Begin by responding to the supervisee's answer, "You're saying _____" or "So you feel _____." Then reflect on, or think carefully about, the response you receive to your statement.

The person may be leveling with you and giving you the information you need to manage things or even to provide assistance. The person might be leveling with you as best as he or she can, but is perhaps not giving you all the information you need. Or he or she may be covering something up, which means that the person is still not fully open—still not really communicating with you. Your observation skills are critical here.

REFLECTING means thinking about what you have—and haven't—learned.

How does he look?	In reflecting on the person's answer to your question, you can think about four specific things: How does he look as he answers (e.g., relaxed, uncomfortable); what is he doing while he answers (e.g., facing you and making eye contact, looking away, looking down at his feet); what has he actually said (e.g., the information content of his answer); and what has he failed to say (e.g., any "gaps" in the way the answer fits with your questions)? By reflecting on these four areas of concern, you can make sure that you fully understand all the implications of the answer. Once you have responded to this answer, you can ask additional questions to get the rest of the information you need. By using your basic skills—responding, asking good questions, reflecting, and then responding again—you'll be recycling.
What's he doing?	
What did he say?	
What didn't he say?	
Recycling	

Example	You are a female sergeant in the C.I.A. Let's imagine that you're talking with a young ex-con who hasn't been out of prison too long. You recognize that he's really scared stiff because of the pressure he's getting from some group on the street. You're able to respond to him at the level of feeling and meaning: "So you really feel scared because these guys just want to take you right over." Now you're set to ask a question: "Who are the guys who have been hassling you the most?" The ex-con looks around quickly, then down at his feet. When his answer comes, it is given in a low, unclear voice: "Oh, just some of the guys from the old neighborhood."

You look at his appearance and see he's really uptight. He won't look you in the eye—he won't even speak up in a clear voice. On top of this, he has answered your questions with only the vaguest kind of information. In the end, his answer gives you nothing.

Upon reflection, you realize that this guy is not only scared in general, but is really frightened right now, like he doesn't want to be seen talking to you. In other words, your reflecting lets you know that this isn't a guy who's trying to play it smart with you. He's not clamming up on purpose. Instead, he's just living in fear right there in front of you. Realizing all of this, you're able to respond even more fully and immediately to him: "You're scared stiff right now because whoever's hassling you might get wind of us talking together." And the ex-con looks up, surprised. He didn't know any officer could really see and hear him as he actually is. You've just grown about six inches in his eyes—maybe to the point where you suddenly seem stronger than the threat of those who have been hassling him. Instead of clamming up, the young man keeps on talking, answering your next questions more fully, which is just what you want him to do, because in the end, you know you gained his confidence and learned the information you needed to get.

VIDEO **"Asking Relevant Questions: The Wrong Way and the Right Way"**

ROLE-PLAY ACTIVITY	Supervisee	Supervisor	Group
	1) Role plays stimulus **2)** Reacts to responses and answers questions **3)** Gives feedback	**1)** Positions Postures Observes Listens **2)** Pauses and responds to feeling and/or meaning **3)** Asks questions after responding (5WH) **4)** Pauses, reflects on answer to question	**1)** Positions Postures Observes Listens **2)** Writes own responses and questions **3)** Rates supervisor's response **4)** Rates question "Yes/No" **5)** Presents each response and question **6)** Gives feedback on asking questions **7)** Reflects on choice of response: Would it have warranted both feeling and meaning?

Jimmy was an inmate who everyone—officers and other inmates alike—invariably referred to as "a bad mother." There was a lot of respect in this phrase. You learned respect around Jimmy. How could you help it? He was 6 feet 5 inches, 275 pounds, and a former sergeant in the Green Berets. To top it off, he had a temper like a bear just coming out of hibernation who found the ground was still frozen solid.

Jimmy didn't like officers. In his time, he'd sent more than a few to the hospital. By now, the officers had figured out a drill. When they wanted Jimmy out of his cell, six of them went in and brought him out. Even then, it wasn't easy.

One day a lieutenant who had been assigned to the street came on to begin his duty as the police department detention administrator. The "old hands" were happy to show him around. "Listen," they said. "You gotta meet Jimmy."

"Jimmy?" The lieutenant didn't have a whole lot of experience in handling persons in the department lockup, but he knew a set-up when he saw one. Half a dozen seasoned officers accompanied the lieutenant to Jimmy's cell, grinning and nudging each other. Oh, they wouldn't let the lieutenant get hurt or anything, they just wanted to know if the lieutenant had been walking the street too long.

"Hey, Jimmy—you got someone to see you," one of the officers told the huge inmate, unlocking the cell and moving back quickly. "You said you wanted to talk to the new direc-tor of the lockup."

Jimmy's only answer was a grunt. He had been sleeping. Now he emerged slowly from his bunk scowling and rubbing his eyes.

"What do you miserable creeps want now? Man, I'm gonna tear somebody into small pieces if you come close enough!" His eyes focused on the lieutenant for the first time. "What's this, some kinda bait or somethin'?"

The older officers expected the lieutenant to back off when he saw Jimmy towering over him. Instead, the new man stuck out his hand.

"I'm Lieutenant Ben Jones," he said. "I guess you're really ripped at us for just barging in on you."

The other officers saw Jimmy's brow furrow. He'd been about to swing and they'd been all tensed up to jump in. But now Jimmy seemed unsure. He didn't shake. But he also didn't swing.

Then his face cleared. In another moment he flung his head back and laughed out loud. "Whooeee!" He calmed down at last and looked at the lieutenant. "I knew it! I knew if I just hung around this place long enough they'd have to send in a real human being to handle me!"

And that was it. In choosing to initiate communication instead of using force, the lieutenant had taken Jimmy off guard. This was a new approach. More than that, it was an indication to an inmate full of anger and hostility that maybe there still were people out there who could talk to him—even listen to him. And that knowledge made all the difference in the world to Jimmy!

What enabled the lieutenant to make this kind of difference, of course, was his communication skills—in particular, his ability to respond. And these are the same skills you yourself have begun to master.

In the first section of this manual, you learned the skills that are necessary to size up a situation. Now, working through this second section, you've learned the skills you need in order to initiate meaningful communication to improve your management potential—the skills involved in responding and asking questions. These skills are designed to help you manage by using communication skills. The payoffs are always good for all concerned. Now it's time to move on—to go beyond sizing up and communicating—and consider what's involved in really controlling the situation. We'll concentrate on this topic, and the skills it requires, in the final section of this manual.

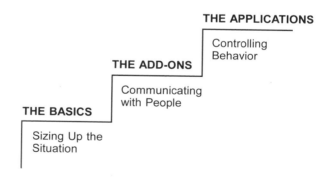

THE APPLICATIONS

Controlling Behavior

THE ADD-ONS

Communicating with People

THE BASICS

Sizing Up the Situation

Section III

The Applications:
Controlling Behavior

The application skills combine the basic and the add-on skills, and are aimed at controlling behavior. These skills are important in helping you maintain control and manage people well.

The applications include three specific skills:

THE APPLICATIONS

Controlling Behavior

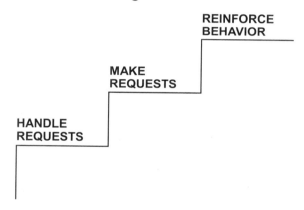

Example   Lieutenant Steve Kelly has a reputation for applying the rules when they suit him and always saying, "No," just because he feels like it.

Steve has been married to his wife, June, for 18 years. Both of their children moved out of the house following high school. June informed Steve that she wanted a divorce now that the children were gone.

75

She told Steve their marriage, for the most part, was a failure due to Steve's over-controlling nature and his know-it-all attitude toward her and the children.

Steve was shocked. He knew they had problems, but not to the point of divorce.

One evening, Steve was drinking at his favorite bar. He was down in the dumps. June had just moved out, leaving him alone in the house. Steve, knowing that he had had too much to drink, called three fellow officers for a ride home. All three of them said they were busy and suggested he take a cab.

Steve became angry after the third officer told him no. The officer told him that he was off duty and there was no obligation to pick him up. Steve decided to drive his vehicle home despite having a few drinks.

Approximately 5 minutes from home, he was stopped by a state trooper. Steve got out of his car and identified himself as a police lieutenant. Steve was expecting "officer courtesy" from a fellow officer.

The trooper wanted to see proof of insurance and Steve's driver's license. Steve refused, stating who he was. The trooper was young and "by the book." He told Steve he didn't care who he was. Steve became irate and a scuffle ensued between him and the trooper.

Eventually, some back-up troopers arrived, and Steve was booked for DUI and placed in the county lockup. He was also charged with resisting arrest.

The moral of this story is not that Steve should have been given officer courtesy, but that Steve's management style of people had been arbitrary his whole life. Yet, when Steve experienced someone like himself, he became angry and combative. If Steve had developed effective social intelligence skills earlier in his career, he might have prevented the above. He might have preserved his marriage and family. He might also have ensured that any fellow officer would grant his needs when he needed them, whether on or off duty. Steve's poor controlling skills of him and others led to his demise.

Controlling is key

Controlling behavior simply means taking charge. This is what it's all about in law enforcement. Without the ability to control behavior, all the other efforts are wasted. A supervisor has to do everything he or she can to ensure appropriate behavior in the interests of society, in themselves, and in the interest of supervisees. The same holds true for all of us. Learning to control our behavior is in our interest. Without control, nothing productive can, or will, occur.

This section of the manual builds on previous sections. It explains how to control behavior by using good management skills.

WHAT ARE THE SKILLS?

In this final section of the manual, we'll take a close look at three different areas of skills. These skills are dealt with here as "applications" because they really represent the specific ways in which you can apply all of the other skills you've developed in order to manage and control behavior in the most effective possible manner:

Three application skills

- Handling requests
- Making requests
- Reinforcing behavior

Unlike the earlier skills in Sections I and II, these three areas are not all cumulative—you will be involved at any given time in either handling requests or making requests of your own. In either situation, however, you will want to reinforce the desired behaviors in order to increase the chances that they will reoccur.

Before going any further, let's take a look at a couple of these skills in action.

Example Here is a routine situation where a supervisor demonstrates skill in management. It involves both the law enforcement supervisee making a request and, in turn, a request being handled by his supervisor.

Sgt. Joan Wilson: Larry, I'd like you to switch your shift with Paul for the next two weeks because Paul has been having problems with his neck and can't ride.

Officer Larry Wright: Is it okay with you if I try to get someone else to do it? I'd like to keep my schedule as it is since I started bowling in a league.

Sgt. Joan Wilson: I'm sorry, Larry, I know that would upset your schedule, but I can't use anyone else since you are the only one who can switch in your unit. I've already checked it out with the other guys. It will only be until Paul's neck gets better or we transfer him.

Officer Larry Wright: Why do you always pick on me? I'm always the one who gets screwed on these deals.

Sgt. Joan Wilson: I know this irritates the hell out of you because it will interrupt your routine, but it's the best I can do right now. Please report at 10:00 a.m. tomorrow instead of 2:00 p.m.

Control through skill The sergeant in this case used her skills to control this situation. She didn't demean or put down, and she didn't use sarcasm. You will observe, however, that included in her skills were firmness and reasons for her actions. There was no weakness. The officer now knows *what* he is expected to do and *why*. The sergeant was even able to continue to be responsive to the officer when the officer became irritated. Using these skills gets the job done and increases the probability that the officer will feel he has been treated fairly, even if he has to have his routine interrupted.

PRACTICE Why is control important for management?

_____

_____

_____

What does a supervisee gain when he or she learns to control his or her own behavior?

_____

_____

_____

79

Handling Requests

Handling requests is the ability to manage requests in a fair and effective manner. The skillful handling of requests helps build trust and reduce tension.

The two steps in handling requests are:

INTERVENTION
MODEL

THE APPLICATIONS

Controlling Behavior

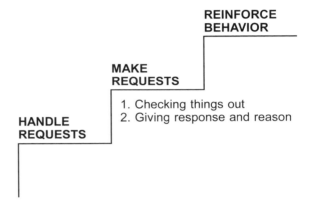

REINFORCE BEHAVIOR

MAKE REQUESTS

1. Checking things out
2. Giving response and reason

HANDLE REQUESTS

Rules, regulations, and rights

Before we turn to the skills involved in handling requests, we should spend a minute reviewing the way in which rules and regulations often relate to the specific things to which people do—and do not—have a right.

Although times are changing rapidly, each officer is bound by certain legal and departmental requirements to provide certain things to society. Most of these things are seen to be basic rights and/or needs to which all citizens, and your supervisees, are entitled. You probably have written regulations (not always up-to-date ones) to guide you in these areas. Abiding by these rights and needs usually enables a supervisor to establish a working relationship with most supervisees and, if applicable, citizens.

There is always that 10 to 20 percent who react negatively no matter what you do. But by following the regulations, you can usually expect people to comply. You have taken away excuses for negative behavior, even in the eyes of people who want to see you as unfair or arbitrary.

PART 1 OF
HANDLING
REQUESTS

Checking out the person and situation. While responding to any request, you need to use your basic skills to check out the person who makes it. Is this person leveling with you, or is he or she trying to play some kind of game? You also need to check out the situation in terms of any policies or regulations that might apply. Using your positioning, observing, listening, and responding skills will be invaluable to you here. As you practice, this will become very clear to you.

CHECKING THINGS OUT involves
sizing up the person and/or situation.

Legitimate
or not?

It goes without saying that you are, and will be, receiving requests from people. Some will be legitimate, some will not. Each request must be responded to. Even if you choose to ignore a request, you have responded to it, and some consequence will occur that can affect your ability to handle and control people. If you find this hard to believe, put yourself in a situation where you want your shift supervisor to consider one of your own requests, and you are ignored.

81

1) How might you feel if a request was important to you and it was denied?

Feeling Word:

_____

2) What message would it communicate if it happened often?

_____

_____

_____

3) How might it affect your performance?

_____

_____

_____

CHECKING OUT REQUESTS involves deciding if the requests are legitimate or not.

Sometimes there will be situations where circumstances cannot be handled by regulations or rules. They may require the following questions to be asked before granting or not granting a request:

- Does a basic need/right apply to the request (beyond policy and procedure)?

    Example: *The supervisee must deal with a life or death emergency.*

82

- Does the supervisee's special circumstances or past performance apply to the request?

  Example: *The supervisee has a history of doing good work and rarely makes requests that could override rules and regulations.*

- Are there situational circumstances beyond rules and regulations that might apply to granting or not granting the request?

  Example: *If you force the application of the rules or regulations, you make matters worse for everyone concerned (you, the requestor, and the organization as a whole).*

Keep in mind

Rules and regulations are necessary because they provide guidelines for everyone to follow without personal emotions or perceptions affecting the request response.

On the other hand, the application of rules and regulations has the potential for making matters worse. This is because rules and regulations cannot list every exception to the rule or predict circumstances that require flexibility.

Also keep in mind that as a manager, if you circumvent a rule or regulation that causes a bigger problem, you are accountable.

PRACTICE Read the following situations. Then describe how you would check them out.

Officer Request: Lieutenant Smith, can I leave early today to pick up my child? My wife can't do it.

What skills would be important to use in this situation?

_____

_____

What rules or regulations must be considered?

_____

_____

A citizen makes this request after demanding to see someone in charge:

Elderly Citizen Request: Sergeant Jones, your Officer Walker was rude to me today when he came to my house. He told me it wasn't his job to get my cat out of the tree in the front yard.

What skills would be important to use in this situation?

_____

_____

What rules or regulations must be considered?

_____

_____

By knowing which of the sizing-up and communicating skills to use, you can ensure that you really know what's happening with a particular person who is making a request. And by reviewing the appropriate rules and regulations, you'll have a good idea of whether the request is, or is not, legitimate. Now you're ready to respond to the request itself.

Checking Things Out Summary

1) Use basic skills: arrange, position, posture, observe, listen.

2) Use add-ons, if applicable: respond and ask relevant questions.

3) Know policies and procedures that apply to the request.

4) Ask: Does a basic need/right apply to the request?

5) Ask: Does the supervisee's special circumstances or past performance apply to the request?

6) Are there situational factors that apply to the request?

Now you're ready to respond to the request itself.

Responding with a reason for your decision. The new skill here involves indicating the action you're going to take (i.e., your decision) and giving the person your reason. Giving the supervisee or citizen a good reason for your decision is not a sign of weakness. On the contrary, it is the best way to minimize future complaints. If you turn the supervisee or citizen down, they won't be able to complain that you didn't tell them why. And if you grant their request, they'll know that it was just for this one situation and for a good and clear reason.

RESPONDING with a reason
eliminates possible hassles.

Reasons for action

Basically, a supervisor has three possible avenues of action in relation to a request. In each case, they should give some reason for their action. Here are some formats that can be used:

"Yes"   "Yes, I'll do (it) _____ because _____."

"No"   "No, I won't do (it) _____ because _____."

"I'll check"   "I'll look into (it) _____ because _____, and I will get back to you (when) _____ and (where) _____ with the answer."

How you decide

In each instance, the supervisor bases his or her intent on the laws and regulations that apply. In cases where people request something beyond what they are entitled to by law and regulation, your response may be influenced by the requesting person's behavior (past and present), what is being requested, the way it is asked for, and the information you have gained by checking things out.

For example, a supervisee's spouse asks you, "Can you talk to my husband about our marital problems? He says he's working overtime, and that's why he's not coming home." You know he hasn't been working overtime.

Take care of basic rights

While a supervisor may have an option in a case like the one above, some things—like responding to a supervisee in distress—cannot be denied. You may have options with an abusive citizen who demands attention, but you can't deny that citizen emergency service when it is warranted. Knowing the law and the regulations of your department will definitely make your job easier—especially with all the grievances that are initiated these days. Yet, by taking care of the basic rights/needs of citizens and supervisees, tensions will be greatly reduced.

Taking care of basic rights/needs is a must in any relationship. It would be very hard for a citizen or supervisee to believe you wanted to assist them if you did not attend to their basic rights/needs (i.e., if you did not give them what they were entitled to—sometimes beyond policy/roles). Dealing with such rights/needs in a concrete way builds trust that will increase the chances that you will get the support you and your department want from supervisees and citizens.

List four legitimate requests a supervisee could make:

1) _____

2) _____

3) _____

4) _____

List four non-legitimate requests a supervisee could make:

REQUEST	**WHY**
1) _____	_____
2) _____	_____
3) _____	_____
4) _____	_____

List four "maybe" requests a supervisee could make:

REQUEST	**WHY**
1) _____	_____
2) _____	_____
3) _____	_____
4) _____	_____

VIDEO

"Handling Requests: The Wrong Way and the Right Way"

ROLE-PLAY ACTIVITY

Supervisee	Supervisor	Group
1) Gives the setting **2)** Makes request **3)** Gives feedback after group has finished their assignment	**1)** Positions Postures Observes Listens **2)** Checks things out: responds, asks relevant questions **3)** Pauses 30 seconds to assess request (legitimate or not) **4)** Gives action plus reason	**1)** Positions Postures Observes Listens **2)** Checks things out **3)** Rates supervisor: a) action plus reason "Yes/No"; b) action and reason; if no, why? **4)** Gives action plus response for feedback

Making Requests

Making requests is the ability to manage people by making specific requests of them. Making requests skillfully improves the chances that people will cooperate and more readily carry out your requests.

The two steps in making requests are:

THE APPLICATIONS

Controlling Behavior

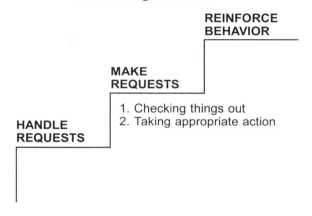

REINFORCE
BEHAVIOR

MAKE
REQUESTS

1. Checking things out
2. Taking appropriate action

HANDLE
REQUESTS

The two procedures involved in making requests in an effective way are checking things out (using the same procedures as when you are handling requests) and taking appropriate action. As before, you need to check things out to ensure that you don't make the wrong move—a move that might increase tension rather than calm things down. Once you've done this, you can decide whether the best action will involve a simple request, an order, or even direct physical action.

Know the
situation

Use basic skills

Checking things out. Since the procedures here will be the same as those involved in handling requests, there's no need to go back over them at length. Here, however, your aim should be to understand as much as possible about the situation involving the person who you plan to have do something: Are they with family members/friends? Are they someone you've had prior problems with? Will they feel they're losing face if you give them an order and, therefore, react antagonistically? Are they in the midst of doing something, and now you will be interrupting them? By using your basic sizing-up and responding skills, you can increase the chances that you will make a request that a person or people will respond to without increasing tension.

CHECKING THINGS OUT involves
the use of your basic and responding skills
and skills applicable to handling requests.

Taking appropriate action. Making requests of supervisees is obviously a routine part of supervising people. Many requests are made during each shift, but we often find that little thought is given to how these requests will impact both the short- and long-term responses and cooperation of supervisees. As many of you know, it's how the request is made that often makes the difference, not the nature of the request.

TAKING ACTION means selecting
the best way to make your request.

91

How you ask may mean more than what you ask! In taking action to get a supervisee to do something, remember that you have to be specific. You should identify what you want done and when. By being clear and concise, you greatly reduce the opportunities for confusion and misinterpretation about what you want done.

Many supervisors have found that a polite request is effective in getting supervisees to do as they have been requested. However, there are some supervisors who feel that supervisees don't deserve politeness, or that being polite makes a supervisor look weak. In reality, everyone—including your most difficult supervisees—deserves the opportunity to have requests made of them in a respectful and polite manner. You set the standard. By being polite, even under the most difficult circumstances, you are showing your strength, maturity, and clear thinking. And when a supervisee doesn't do something reasonable when asked politely, it is the supervisee who looks weak, not you.

Mild or polite format A mild (polite) request can take the form: "Would you (please) _____" or it can take the form "I would appreciate it if you would _____." When you make a request, the most direct method is simply to identify what you desire and then use the format "I want you to _____." **Direct format** But because people often resent authority if you are simply telling them to do something, you may have fewer hassles if you use more of a polite/mild request format. Examples might be "I'd like you to do _____" or "Would you stop _____?"

Softening a request You can soften the statement even more by using polite words. For example, "I'd like you to *please* stop _____." What format you use for making a request will depend on the situation and the particular supervisee. Of course, if the mild method doesn't work, you always have the option of moving to a stronger position, including a direct order. But, most experienced supervisors agree that, in the long haul, it is generally better if direct confrontation can be avoided.

Get stronger when necessary

Making Request Formats

Mild: "Would you (request) because (reason)."

Moderate: "I want you to (request) because (reason)."

Strong (Immediate Action): "I want you to (request) now."

Use responding skills

You may also want to use your responding skills when taking action. For example, you come across a supervisee who is in a place where he should not be. You **position** yourself so that you can see him but he cannot see you. You **observe** for a little while because he appears to be doing nothing wrong. Then you move into **position** so that he can see you. As you approach, you recognize the person. He, in fact, gives you a greeting: "Hello." You give him the benefit of the doubt in the sense that you are open to what he is going to say. The person is a new employee to the area and you haven't seen or heard anything to make you more than routinely cautious. You make your request:

Example **Supervisor:** Hi! This is a restricted area.
(Moderate) You'll have to leave it right now.

New I just wanted to get off by myself
Employee: for a while.

Supervisor: I can appreciate your wanting some privacy, but you can't be in this area without authorization.

PRACTICE There may be times when you want to start right out with a direct order or take immediate action. List two examples of when you would give a direct order or when you would take immediate action without making a request. Give the reason why you would do this.

Direct Order

Situation 1: _____

_____

Situation 2: _____

_____

Take Immediate Action

Situation 1: _____

_____

Situation 2: _____

_____

VIDEO **"Making Requests: The Wrong Way and the Right Way"**

Supervisee	Supervisor	Group
1) Says "no" to the request, and refuses to give a reason **2)** Argues	**1)** Positions Postures **2)** Makes a legitimate request of the supervisee **3)** Checks things out: Observes Listens Responds Asks questions **4)** Escalates the request; makes it more directive	**1)** Positions Postures Observes Listens **2)** Records own version of request and why it should be made **3)** Rates supervisor "Yes/No" on content and style of request, then gives own version of request

95

Reinforcing Behavior

We reinforce desirable behaviors that we want to keep occurring or occur more often, and we punish undesirable behaviors that we want to occur less often, or maybe not at all.

The four steps of reinforcing behavior are:

THE APPLICATIONS

Controlling Behavior

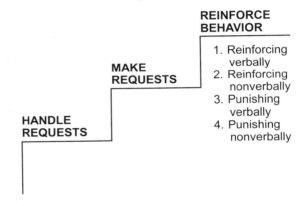

In general, people perform behaviors that give them a good feeling, and they typically avoid behaviors that make them feel uncomfortable. The problem is that we often experience those good feelings (i.e., feel rewarded) for behaviors that are undesirable or inappropriate. For example, criminals who go uncaught are reinforced by the attention and material gain. Parents often reinforce complaining children in grocery stores by giving them sweets. Some police officers receive the adulation of their peers for their use of force. In these examples, the rewards that accompany the criminal behavior, the public com

96

plaining, and the use of force almost certainly guarantee that these behaviors will continue, and maybe increase, in frequency.

Being a supervisor or manager means that you have the opportunity to change the behaviors of your supervisees using some fundamental skills of **reinforcing** those behaviors you want to maintain or increase and **punishing** those behaviors you want to decrease or eliminate. Using reinforcement and punishment appropriately can enhance the likelihood of responsible behavior from supervisees immediately while working toward long-term outcomes such as supervisee cooperation and support.

Note: The better the rapport that you have with the supervisee, the more efficient and effective your reinforcing and punishing will be in shaping his or her behavior.

Two kinds of reinforcement   Reinforcement refers to the use of rewards to maintain or increase desired behaviors. Reinforcement can be given by both verbal and nonverbal feedback to supervisees.

REINFORCING means using verbal and/or nonverbal responses as ways to maintain and/or increase desired behaviors.

Verbal reinforcement   Verbal reinforcement means saying something with the intention of maintaining or increasing a desired behavior. Most of the time, the words we choose are experienced as pleasant by the person we're talking to. We've all heard or said these phrases: "Bob, thank you for always being prompt with your report," or "John, I appreciated you taking the responsibility for that without being asked," or "Susie, great job!"

Unfortunately, we are probably also familiar with words or phrases that are *not* experienced as pleasant but are still aimed at maintaining or increasing a desired behavior. For example, when a supervisee, Officer Williams, asked her supervisor if he got her shift report, he replied, "Of course I did. What are you looking for, a compliment? That's your job." The manager's intent may have been to maintain or increase the behavior of completing an on-time shift report, but his response probably didn't leave the supervisee with a very pleasant feeling.

Which response would you prefer: "Great job with that shift report. Thanks!" or "That's your job!"

VIDEO — **"Reinforcing Behavior Verbally: The Wrong Way and the Right Way"**

Nonverbal reinforcement

Nonverbal reinforcement means using non-verbal cues to maintain or increase desired behaviors. The most obvious nonverbal cues are smiling, nodding the head, giving a pat on the back, etc. A person moving his vehicle to provide a larger space for better pedestrian movement and getting a nod and a smile is an example of nonverbal reinforcement. Again, these are examples that will most likely leave the person with a pleasant feeling.

However, some nonverbal cues might be intended to reinforce a behavior but actually be experienced as less than pleasant. For example, let's look at Officer Williams from the example above. What if she had taken the completed shift report on time to the manager, and he snatched it out of her hands and placed it in his report basket while never making eye contact with her. His intent may have been to reinforce her on-time report writing by showing her what a busy man he is. If you were Officer Williams, what would you think?

VIDEO | **"Reinforcing Behavior Nonverbally: The Wrong Way and the Right Way"**

Punishment Punishment means saying or doing something that is intended to reduce or eliminate an undesirable behavior. Again, this can be done using verbal and/or nonverbal feedback with supervisees.

Although it is generally accepted that punishment is a tool of "last resort" for the effective supervisor or manager, its timing is also determined by other factors such as the nature of the behavior, the context the behavior occurred in, previous displays of the behavior, and the rules and regulations that apply to the behavior, to name only a few. When administered fairly and appropriately, it can be a powerful way to change behaviors.

PUNISHMENT means using verbal and/or nonverbal responses as ways to decrease or eliminate undesirable behaviors.

Verbal punishment Verbal punishment means saying something with the intention of decreasing or eliminating an undesirable behavior. These can be some of your most difficult conversations. Therefore, your ability to size up the situation and use your responding and requesting skills will be invaluable here. And again, being polite can be your best asset. Examples of verbal punishments can be mild, such as, "Please don't do that behavior again," or intense,

99

"Stop it NOW!" They can express feelings, such as, "I'm disappointed that you chose to behave that way," or explanatory, "Let's talk about this behavior. We've talked about this on two previous occasions, and now it's occurred again, so now we're going to talk about the consequences of what you've done."

Making entries in a personnel file that document the behavior and its consequences also fit in the category of verbal punishments.

Insults and hurtful statements are also examples of verbal punishment. "I can't believe you're so stupid that you are still writing that report. Grandma was slow, but she was old! Hurry up!" or "Only an idiot would try to do it that way."

Which of these verbal punishments would you prefer to receive if you had done something inappropriate?

Nonverbal punishment

Nonverbal punishment means using nonverbal cues to decrease or eliminate undesired behaviors. The most obvious nonverbal cues are shaking your head back and forth indicating "no" or "stop," looking at the person with a serious expression to communicate displeasure, and rolling the eyes. Other nonverbal punishments involve removing privileges or assigning the person to undesirable duties.

Some of the less productive nonverbal punishments include slapping, hitting, punching, pinching, and other physically abusive behaviors. The use of obscene and/or exaggerated gestures of disgust, contempt, and displeasure are also considered generally ineffective.

PRACTICE   List some verbal reinforcers you could give as a Sheriff's department supervisor and the behaviors that would warrant them. (Remember that certain written statements are also included in this category, such as an entry into a deputy's personnel file.)

Verbal reinforcers:

1) _____

2) _____

3) _____

4) _____

Behaviors receiving verbal reinforcers:

1) _____

2) _____

3) _____

4) _____

List some nonverbal reinforcers you can administer as a Sheriff's department supervisor and the behaviors that would receive them.

Nonverbal reinforcers:

1) _____

2) _____

3) _____

4) _____

Behaviors receiving nonverbal reinforcers:

1) _____

2) _____

3) _____

4) _____

List some punishments you can administer and the behaviors that would warrant them.

Punishments:

1) _____

2) _____

3) _____

4) _____

Behaviors you might punish:

1) _____

2) _____

3) _____

4) _____

ROLE-PLAY ACTIVITY	Supervisee	Supervisor	Group
ROUND 1	**1)** Gives the setting and trust level in existence **2)** Role plays a desired behavior (e.g., takes the lead on a project, turns in shift report complete and on time, etc.)	**1)** Positions Postures Observes Listens **2)** Responds **3)** Reinforces desired behavior a) Verbally b) Nonverbally	**1)** Responds Observes Listens **2)** Writes own reinforcement and why **3)** Rates supervisor "Yes/No" on correctness of reinforcement. If "No," why?
ROUND 2	**1)** Role plays an undesired behavior (e.g., late for work, turns in shift report late and incomplete, etc.)	**1)** Positions Postures Observes Listens **2)** Responds **3)** Punishes undesired behavior a) Verbally b) Nonverbally	**1)** Responds Observes Listens **2)** Writes own reinforcement and why **3)** Rates supervisor "Yes/No" on correctness of punishment. If "No," why?

Summary of the Applications

You've developed professional skills to do a professional's job. You've helped to lay to rest that familiar stereotype that supervisees have of law enforcement supervisors as being over-authoritarian and uncaring, and having a "just the facts" mentality. And you've gone beyond. You've begun to act on one of the most basic equations in all of human history.

HUMAN ACTIONS DETERMINE HUMAN REACTIONS

The cornerstone of the social intelligence skills you've learned is **decency:** simple human decency. You've got a job to do. But in doing it, you've learned how you can handle people like the human beings they are. And in return, you'll be able to promote more decent and constructive behavior on their part. This process involves what has been called "the principle of reciprocal behavior"— a fancy way of saying that **we all get back what we give.** In your case, you've learned how to invest your work with professional effectiveness—with real skills—and still give people decent treatment.

About the Author

Steve J. Sampson, Ph.D.
Founder, President

Dr. Steve Sampson has been teaching conflict resolution and interpersonal skills for over 30 years. He brings both academic knowledge and practical experience to his seminars.

As an Educator, he holds a Bachelors Degree in Sociology from the University of Massachusetts (1970) and a Masters (1976) and Doctoral Degree (1981) in Counseling Psychology from Georgia State University. He is a nationally recognized Master Trainer in Interpersonal Communication Skills since 1977, and has presented that training to over 300 agencies and organizations in 40 states. He is a former Assistant Professor of Criminal Justice at Georgia State University from 1979 to 1985. More recently, he retired from his position as a Clinical Professor in the Counseling and Psychological Services department at Georgia State University (1995-2004).

As a Licensed Psychologist, he is the former Chief of Psychology of Georgia Regional Hospital, Atlanta, Georgia (1993 to 1995). He is also a nationally recognized counseling psychologist who works with various law enforcement agencies conducting fitness for duty evaluations and post shooting debriefings since 1982. He has been a contract Psychologist with 25 Metropolitan Atlanta Law Enforcement Agencies since 1991.

As a Criminologist, Dr. Sampson is the former correctional superintendent for Massachusetts Halfway Houses Inc. (1969 to 1973), as well as the former Correctional Superintendent for the Georgia Department of Corrections (1974 to 1976). He has provided training to over 250 prisons, law enforcement, and public safety agencies in Social Skills Training since 1977.

As an author, he has published the following books on Social Intelligence Skills:

- *Social Intelligence Skills for Law Enforcement Managers*

- *Social Intelligence Skills for Correctional Managers*
- *Social Intelligence Skills for Government Managers*

He has recently published a new book:

- *How to be in a Personal Relationship*

NOTES

A. Human Technogy

    1 - Study of How/Action

NOTE. Intelligence (To be aware)